THE DESIGN SOURCE BOOK OF

Home Decor

Throws and Pillows
to Knit & Crochet

by

Judith Shangold

featuring

Manos del Uruguay Yarn

Contents

Introduction

It is impossible to publish a book of knitting and crochet designs in the year 2000 without making some comment about our lives as we enter the new millennium. Change is all around us – in the ways we work, conduct business, buy and sell products, communicate with each other. My own reaction is to want to embrace the possibilities offered by these developments and, at the same time, hold on for dear life to what's valuable from my present and past. Though I often find E-mail convenient, and an easier way to stay in contact with people who live at a distance, I still enjoy the more personal contact of a telephone conversation. And though I spend countless hours in front of a computer (designing this book, for instance), I still love to sit down with piles of yarn around me to work on a knitting or crocheting project.

In these changing times, the popularity of home decorating is no surprise. The more things change, the more comfort we seek from our home surroundings. This sophisticated, elegant collection of throws and pillows fits comfortably into today's homes. They add color and warmth to living rooms, porches, dens, bedrooms, children's, and babies' rooms. And because they are made by your own hands, they express your individuality and creativity.

I have designed these projects to be simple and portable. All of the throws, except the Wildflowers Baby Throw, are worked in pieces – easy to take along on business or vacation trips.

The samples are shown in Manos del Uruguay yarn. Spun and hand-dyed in South America using a unique dyeing process, this 100% wool yarn is soft, lustrous, and striated in color. With 85 shades available, the yarn is an artist's and craftsperson's dream. Color combinations are endless. Use your upholstery fabric, wallpaper, or rugs to inspire you. If you are fortunate enough to be near a shop that carries Manos, bring some fabric or paper samples with you when choosing colors. Or use the color card on pages 8 and 9 of this book and contact a mail order supplier. For help in finding a supplier, call our toll free number shown on the back page.

If you wish to substitute other yarns, simply choose some of similar weight that will knit to approximately the same gauge. Or, since fit is not an issue, you may use heavier or thinner yarns. You would have to adjust needle sizes and gauge accordingly and remember that heavier yarn will create a larger throw while thinner yarn will result in a smaller one. Yarn amounts will also vary; you will need more skeins of heavier yarn since it has fewer yards.

I hope these projects inspire you. The process of knitting or crocheting with wonderful materials is, in itself, a pleasure. The finished products will bring comfort and pleasure to you, your friends, and your family for years.

Enjoy —

Judith

Manos del Uruguay

Manos Del Uruguay is a cooperative of spinners, dyers, knitters and weavers.

Established in 1968 as a nonprofit organization, the cooperative

provides work for women in rural areas of Uruguay.

Artisans in forty locations hand spin and dye

this beautiful wool yarn.

Manos yarn is 100% wool and is available in 85 colors.

It is put up in 3.5 oz / 100 gr skeins with
approximately 135 yds / 122 mtrs per skein.

Handwashable following directions on page 10.

Aran weight, it knits at between 3.5 and 4.5 sts
per inch using needle sizes 8-10US / 5-6mm
and crochets at 3 sts per inch using a J / 6mm hook.

Because Manos is hand spun and dyed, each skein is unique.
When working on a single color project, we recommend alternating
2 rows from one skein with 2 rows from another to give an overall blended effect.

11 navy
45 lapis
38 aster
41 thistle
47 cerise
57 raspberry
61 rhubarb
63 heliotrope
60 french blue
62 cornflower
A midnight
C powder
D spruce
E english
51 jade
43 juniper
46 malachite
Q calypso
04 turquoise
36 mallard
29 steel
13 hunter

MANOS
DEL
URUGUAY

26 rosin
32 gasoline
27 petrol
42 marl
49 henna
Z straw
X topaz
U rust
28 copper
M bing cherry
54 brick
48 cherry
V cinnamon
37 thrush
40 goldenrod
55 olive
W persimmon
R firey red
10 red
58 marigold

G coffee
53 mulberry
44 briar
F stone
I quail
30 silica
52 cameo
19 dove
K putty
35 uranium
25 shale
34 oil slick
08 black
64 pewter
31 nickel
T flannel
59 kohl
14 natural

MANOS DEL URUGUAY

01 pink
33 butane
03 lavender
39 cirrus
O rose
50 heather
21 souffle
20 parma
24 blush
22 mist
18 mint
17 cheek

100 agate
101 jungle
102 canyon
103 mar
104 prairie
105 lava
106 autumn
107 sage
108 granite
109 woodland
110 stellar
111 eclipse
112 moss

Finishing

Follow these diagrams for neat, easy finishing. All techniques are worked with the *right* side of your work facing you. Upon completion, steam your work by placing a wet towel on top and lightly touching a hot iron to the towel, or handwash as follows: Fill sink or washing machine with lukewarm water. Add a teaspoon of dishwashing liquid or no rinse wool wash.* Soak for about 15 minutes. *Do not agitate.* Rinse, if necessary, in same temperature water. Run through the spin cycle. Lay flat on towels to dry.

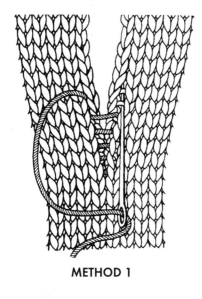

METHOD 1

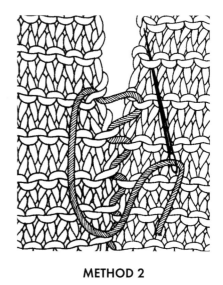

METHOD 2

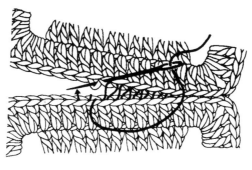

METHOD 3

* available at yarn shops

Glossary

beg = begin, beginning

ch = chain

cn = cable needle

cont = continue, continuing

dec = decrease

dc = double crochet. Yo once, insert hook and draw yarn up – 3 loops on hook, (yo and draw through 2 loops) twice.

foll = follows, following

garter st = knit all rows

inc = increase

K = knit

k2 tog = knit 2 together

LH = left hand

LT = left twist. With the right needle behind the first st, k the 2nd st through back loop, then k the first st through front loop. Drop both sts from left needle.

P = purl

pat = pattern

p2 tog = purl 2 together

rem = remain/ing

rep = repeat

Rev St st = reverse stockinette st. P all RS rows; k all WS rows.

RH = right hand

RS = right side

RT = right twist. K2 tog, leave sts on left needle, k first st again. Sl both sts from needle tog.

sc = single crochet

Shrimp St = work single crochet backwards, i.e., from left to right.

sk = skip

skns = skeins

sl st = slip stitch

sp = space

ssk = Sl 2 sts one at a time as to knit; insert left hand needle into the fronts of these 2 sts from left to right and k2 tog in this position.

st / sts = stitch / stitches

St st = stockinette st. K all RS rows; p all WS rows.

tog = together

tr = triple crochet. Yo twice, insert hook into ring and and draw yarn up – 4 loops on hook, (yo and draw through 2 loops) 3 times.

WS = wrong side

VICTORIAN GARDEN

Directions pages 14–15

Directions pages 16-17

Victorian Garden

Crocheted Puzzle Throw

Pictured page 12

SIZE Throw: 50" x 56" / 125 x 140cm
Baby Throw: 38" x 44" / 95 x 110 cm

MATERIALS Manos del Uruguay. Crochet hook J / 6mm
or size needed to obtain gauge.

	Color	skns	skns/baby	hex	hex/baby
A.	Raspberry 57	2	2	24	24
B.	Thrush 37	1	1	8	8
C.	Uranium 35	5	1	58	12
D.	Oil Slick 34	6	1	72	12
E.	Shale 25	1	0	12	0
F.	Thistle 41	3	3	30	30
G.	Topaz X	1	1	5	5
H.	Mallard 36	2	2	24	24

For alternate colorway, see knitted version on page 16.

GAUGE

1 hexagon measures 4" / 10cm across the widest point.

Hexagons are worked individually. Work number of
hexagons in each color as indicated under materials.

HEXAGON

Ch 7 and join to form a ring with a sl st into first ch.
Rnd 1: 5ch, [tr into ring, 2ch] 11 times, join with a sl st to
3rd ch of first ch-5 – 12 spaces.
Rnd 2: Sl st into next ch-2 space, (3ch, dc, 2ch, 2dc) in same
space, 3dc in next space, *(2dc, 2ch, 2dc) in next space, 3dc in
next space; repeat from * 4 more times. Join with sl st to
3rd ch of ch-3. Fasten off, leaving 6" end.

FINISHING

Sew hexagons together following chart for color arrangement.
Use Seaming Method 3 shown on page 10.

FLOWER PILLOWS See page 61.

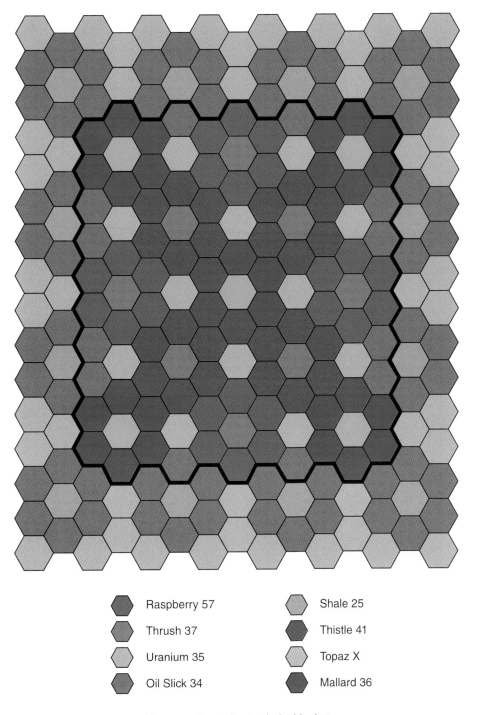

Raspberry 57			Shale 25	
Thrush 37			Thistle 41	
Uranium 35			Topaz X	
Oil Slick 34			Mallard 36	

Heavy outline indicates baby blanket

Cottage Garden

Knitted Puzzle Throw

Pictured page 13

SIZE Throw: 50" x 56" / 125 x 140cm

Baby Throw: 38" x 44" / 95 x 110cm

MATERIALS Manos del Uruguay. Needles size 9US / 5.5mm *or size needed to obtain gauge.* Crochet hook H / 4.75mm.

	Color	skns	skns/baby
A.	Cornflower 62	2	2
B.	Mint 18	1	1
C.	Spruce D	5	1
D.	Cirrus 39	6	1
E.	Powder C	1	0
F.	Rhubarb 61	3	3
G.	Parma 20	1	1
H.	Blush 24	2	2

For alternate colorway, see crocheted version on pages 14–15.

GAUGE 4 sts = 1" / 2.5cm in garter st

1 hexagon measures 4" / 10cm at the widest point.

HEXAGON

Cast on 11 sts.

Row 1(WS): P2, k7, p2

Row 2: K11.

Row 3: P2, yo, k7, yo, p2 – 13 sts.

Row 4: K13

Row 5: P2, k9, p2.

Row 6: K2, yo, k9, yo, k2 – 15 sts.

Row 7: P2, k11, p2.

Row 8: K15.

Row 9: P2, yo, k11, yo, p2 – 17 sts.

Row 10: K17.

Row 11: P2, k13, p2.

Row 12: K2, yo, k13, yo, k2 – 19 sts.

Row 13: P2, k15, p2.

Row 14: K19.

Row 15: P1, p2 tog, yo, ssk, k9, ssk, yo, p2 tog-b, p1 – 17 sts.

Row 16: K17.

Row 17: P2, k13, p2.

Row 18: K1, ssk, yo, ssk, k7, k2 tog, yo, k2 tog, k1 – 15 sts.

Row 19: P2, k11, p2.

Row 20: K15.

Row 21: P1, p2 tog, yo, ssk, k5, ssk, yo, p2 tog-b, p1 – 13 sts.

Row 22: K13.

Row 23: P2, k9, p2.

Row 24: K1, ssk, yo, ssk, k3, k2 tog, yo, k2 tog, k1 – 11 sts.

Row 25: P2, k7, p2.

STRIPS Work strips 1–15 following diagram. Work first hexagon with color indicated. *Cut yarn. With new color, k 1 row. Repeat rows 1–25. Rep from * until strip is complete. Bind off.

FINISHING Sew strips together using Seaming Method 1 shown on page 10. With C, work row of single crochet along top and bottom edge.

Building Blocks

revisited

THE DESIGN SOURCE BOOK OF

Home Decor

DESIGN SOURCE

PO Box 770, Medford, MA 02155

888.566.9970

THE DESIGN SOURCE BOOK OF

Home Decor

Building Blocks revisited

directions on page 51

To create this re-colored version,
use the following materials:

Manos Del Uruguay yarn

Colors

A. Olive 55

B. Bing Cherry M

C. Thistle 41

D. Cinnamon V

E. Heather 50

THE DESIGN SOURCE BOOK OF

Home Decor

Baby Blocks revisited

Finished measurement: 52" X 48"

To create this re-colored and re-sized version, follow directions for blocks starting p.46 and use the following materials:

Manos Del Uruguay yarn

Colors	skns
A. Briar 44	2
B. Shale 25	3
C. Dove 19	2
D Uranium 35	3
E. Mulberry 53	3
F. Putty K	2

DESIGN SOURCE
888.566.9970

Starting at lower edge, work 9 vertical strips as shown in diagram.
For each strip, follow these steps:

1. With first color, cast on 24 sts. K 2 rows.
2. K next row, inc or dec sts to desired number of sts for block.
3. Work block.
4. K next row, inc or dec to 24 sts.
5. K 2 rows.
6. With next color, k 3 rows.

Repeat from Step 2 to end of last block. K next row, inc or dec to 24 sts. K 2 rows. Bind off.

Example: I A = Work Block I on p.46 with color A as listed below.

I A	II B	IV C	V D	II E	V D	IV C	II B	I A
II B	IV C	V D	II E	III B	II E	V D	IV C	II B
IV C	V D	II E	III B	IV F	III B	II E	V D	IV C
V D	II E	III B	IV F	V D	IV F	III B	II E	V D
II E	III B	IV F	V D	Center A	V D	IV F	III B	II E
V D	II E	III B	IV F	V D	IV F	III B	II E	V D
IV C	V D	II E	III B	IV F	III B	II E	V D	IV C
II B	IV C	V D	II E	III B	II E	V D	IV C	II B
I A	II B	IV C	V D	II E	V D	IV C	II B	I A

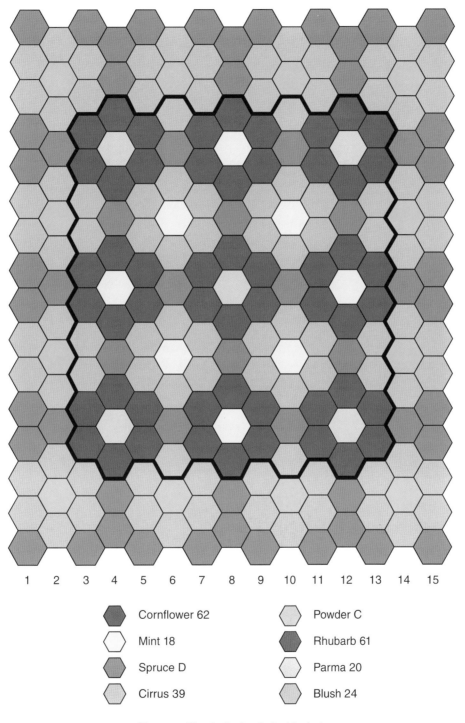

1 2 3 4 5 6 7 8 9 10 11 12 13 14 15

Cornflower 62		Powder C
Mint 18		Rhubarb 61
Spruce D		Parma 20
Cirrus 39		Blush 24

Heavy outline indicates baby blanket

Puzzle

Design your own

Hexagons can be arranged into many different patterns. Here are a few possibilities.
Photocopy several copies of page 18 and use color pencils to experiment with colors and patterns.
Working with one color at a time allows you to see patterns emerge.

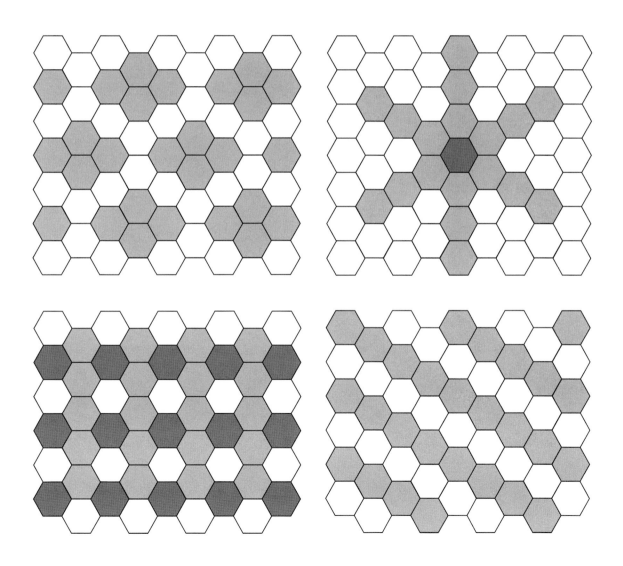

Rock Garden

SIZE Approx. 45" x 60" / 114 x 152cm

MATERIALS Manos Del Uruguay. Crochet hook J / 6mm *or size needed to obtain gauge.*

	Color	skns/blocks		Color	skns/blocks
A.	Granite 108	2	E.	Nickel 31	1
B.	Flannel T	2	F.	Kohl 59	1
C.	Quail I	2	G.	Olive 55	1
D.	Stone F	2	H.	Thrush 37	1
Trim: Black 08		2			

NOTE Throw is made up of 12 blocks. Each block requires 1 skein of yarn and will measure approx. 15" / 38cm square when completed.

GAUGE 3dc = 1" / 2.5cm

BLOCK

Base ring: 5ch, join with sl st.

Rnd 1: 5ch (count as 1dc and 2ch), [3dc into ring, 2ch] 3 times, 2dc into ring, sl st to 3rd of ch-5 – 3dc each side.

Rnd 2: Sl st into corner sp, 7ch (count as 1dc and 4ch), 2dc into same sp, [1dc into each dc across side of square, 2dc into next corner sp, 4ch, 2dc into same corner] 3 times, 1 dc into each dc across side, 1dc into same corner sp as 7dc, sl st to 3rd ch of ch-7 – 7dc each side.

Rep rnd 2 until yarn runs out, end beg of rnd. Set aside.

Make 12 blocks as indicated under materials. Subtract rnds as necessary so that all blocks have the same number of rnds. With trim color, work edging around each block as follows: Work 1sc in each st and 5sc into each corner sp. Sl st to first sc. Cut yarn and pull end through loop.

FINISHING

Follow diagram for color placement. Sew blocks together using Seaming Method 3 on page 10. Join trim color and work 1 rnd of single crochet around entire outside edge.

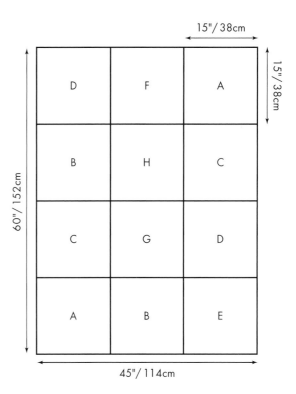

Harvest

SIZE 39" x 52" / 99 x 132cm

MATERIALS Manos del Uruguay, 3 skns each colors A, B, C, D, E, F and 1 extra skein for fringe. Knitting needles size 9US / 5.5 mm *or size needed to obtain gauge*. Crochet hook size H / 4.75mm for fringe.

Yarn amounts are given assuming colors are used as indicated on chart. Throw requires 1 skn each for blocks 2, 3, 5, 8, 10, and 11 and 2 skns each for blocks 1, 4, 6, 7, 9 and 12.

Colorway 1 (p.22)

A. Bing Cherry M
B. Cherry 48
C. Cinnamon V
D. Brick 54
E. Rust U
F. Henna 49
Fringe: D

Colorway 2 (p.27)

Spruce D
Cirrus 39
Steel 29
Jade 51
Stone F
Mallard 36
C

GAUGE 16 sts = 4" / 10cm in pat sts

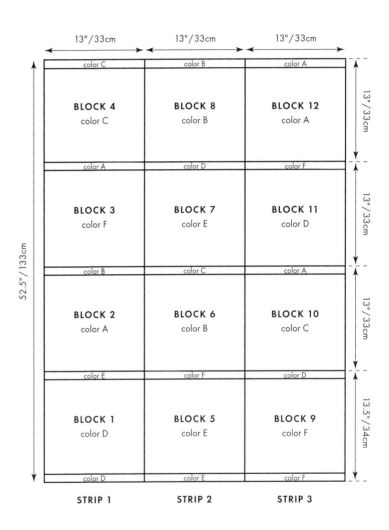

| 13"/33cm | 13"/33cm | 13"/33cm |

| color C | color B | color A |
| **BLOCK 4** color C | **BLOCK 8** color B | **BLOCK 12** color A | 13"/33cm
| color A | color D | color F |
| **BLOCK 3** color F | **BLOCK 7** color E | **BLOCK 11** color D | 13"/33cm
| color B | color C | color A |
| **BLOCK 2** color A | **BLOCK 6** color B | **BLOCK 10** color C | 13"/33cm
| color E | color F | color D |
| **BLOCK 1** color D | **BLOCK 5** color E | **BLOCK 9** color F | 13.5"/34cm
| color D | color E | color F |

52.5"/133cm

STRIP 1   STRIP 2   STRIP 3

STRIP 1

BLOCK 1

With color D, cast on 52 sts. K 4 rows, inc 1 st on last row – 53 sts. Work in pats as follows: **Next Row (RS):** Work 3 sts in **Garter**, 47 sts in **Popcorn**, 3 sts in **Garter**. Cont in pats as established until block measures 13"/33 cm from beg, end with row 2. Change to color E and k 4 rows, dec 1 st on first row and inc 5 sts evenly across last row – 57 sts. Cut yarn.

Popcorn (multiple of 5 sts plus 2)
Row 1 (RS): Knit.
Rows 2 and 4: Purl.
Row 3: K3, *K into front, back, front, back and front of st; with LH needle, lift 5th st on RH needle over first 4 sts; in same way, lift 4th, 3rd, then 2nd st over first st (popcorn made), k4; rep from *, ending last rep k3.
Rep rows 1–4 for Popcorn pat.

BLOCK 2

With color A, cont working on 57 sts from Block 1 as follows:
Next Row (RS): Work 3 sts in **Garter**, 51 sts in **Ripple**, 3 sts in **Garter**. Cont in pats as established until block measures 12½"/32 cm, end with WS row. Change to color B and k 4 rows, dec 5 sts evenly across first row and inc 10 sts across last row – 62 sts. Cut yarn.

Ripple (multiple of 8 sts plus 3)
Row 1 (RS): K2, *k3, p1, k4; rep from *, end last rep k5 instead of k4.
Row 2: P2, *p2, k3, p3; rep from *, end last rep p4 instead of p3.
Row 3: K2, *k1, p2, k1, p2, k2; rep from *, end last rep k3 instead of k2.
Row 4: P2, *k2, p3, k2, p1; rep from *, end last rep p2 instead of p1.
Row 5: K2, *p1, k5, p1, k1; rep from *, end last rep k2 instead of k1.
Row 6: Purl.
Rep rows 1–6 for Ripple pat.

BLOCK 3

With color F, cont working on 62 sts from Block 2 as follows:
Next Row (RS): Work 3 sts in **Garter**, 56 sts in **Triangles**, 3 sts in **Garter**. Cont in pats as established, until block measures 12½"/32 cm, end with WS row. Change to color A and k 4 rows, dec 10 sts evenly across first row and inc 14 sts across last row – 66 sts. Cut yarn.

Triangles (multiple of 5 sts plus 1)
Row 1 (RS): Knit.
Row 2: P1, *k4, p1; rep from *.
Row 3: K1, *p3, k2; rep from *.
Row 4: *P3, k2; rep from *, end p1.
Row 5: K1, *p1, k4; rep from *.
Row 6: Purl.
Row 7: K1, *p4, k1; rep from *.
Row 8: *P2, k3; rep from *, end p1.
Row 9: K1, *P2, k3; rep from *.
Row 10: *P4, k1; rep from *, end p1.
Rep rows 1–10 for Triangles pat.

BLOCK 4

With color C, cont on 66 sts from Block 3 as follows:
Next Row (RS): Work 3 sts in **Garter**, 60 sts **Mock Cable**, 3 sts in **Garter**. Cont in pats as established until block measures 12½"/32 cm, end with WS row. K 4 rows, dec 14 sts evenly across first row – 52 sts. Bind off knitwise.

Mock Cable (multiple of 4 sts)
Rows 1 and 5 (RS): P1, *k2, p2; rep from *, end k2, p1.
Rows 2, 4, 6 and 8: K the knit sts and p the purl sts.
Rows 3 and 7: P1, *skip first st, k 2nd st but do not drop from LH needle, k first st, drop both sts from LH needle, p2; rep from *, end k2, p1.

Rep rows 1–8 for Mock Cable pat.

STRIP 2

BLOCK 5

With color E, cast on 52 sts. K 4 rows, inc 3 sts evenly across last row – 55 sts. Work in pats as follows: **Next Row (RS):** Work 3 sts in **Garter**, 49 sts in **Little Pyramids**, 3 sts in **Garter**. Cont in pats as established until piece measures 13"/33 cm from beg, end with WS row. Change to color F and k 4 rows, dec 3 sts evenly across first row and inc 3 sts across last row – 55 sts. Cut yarn.

Little Pyramids (multiple of 6 sts plus 1)
Row 1 (RS): K6, *p1, k5; rep from *, end p1, k6.
Row 2: K2, *p3, k3; rep from *, end p3, k2.
Row 3: P3, *k1, p5; rep from *, end k1, p3.
Row 4: Rep row 3.
Row 5: Rep row 2.
Row 6: Rep row 1.
Rep rows 1–6 for Little Pyramids pat.

BLOCK 6

With color B, cont on 55 sts from Block 5 as follows:
Next row (RS): Work 3 sts in **Garter**, 49 sts in **Rev St st**, 3 sts in **Garter**. Cont as established for 11 rows more. Keeping first and last 3 sts in Garter, work 13 rows of **Two Hearts**. Cont working Garter and Rev St st as established for 29 rows. Keeping first and last 3 sts in **Garter**, work 13 rows of **Center Heart**. Cont working Garter and Rev St st until block measures 12½"/32 cm, end with WS row. Change to color C and k 4 rows, dec 3 sts evenly across first row and inc 9 sts across last row – 61 sts. Cut yarn.

Double inc: [K1 tbl, k1] in one st, then insert LH needle into the vertical strand that runs downward from between the 2 sts just made and k1 tbl into this strand to make a 3rd st.

Work 5 tog: Sl 3 wyib, *pass the 2nd st on RH needle over the first st, sl first st back to LH needle, pass the 2nd st on LH needle over it*, sl st back to RH needle and rep between *'s, p the rem st.

Two Hearts (49 sts)

Row 1 (RS): P11, double inc, p25, double inc, p11 – 53 sts.
Rows 2, 4, 6 and 8: K the knit sts and p the purl sts.
Row 3: P9, *P2tog, k1, double inc, k1, p2tog*, p21; rep between *'s once, p9.
Row 5: P8, *p2tog, k2, double inc, k2, p2tog*, p19; rep between *'s once, p8.
Row 7: P7, *p2tog, k3, double inc, k3, p2tog*, p17; rep between *'s once, p7.
Row 9: P8, *k4, double inc, k4*, p19; rep between *'s once, p8 – 57 sts.
Row 10: K8, *p5, k1, p5*, k19; rep between *'s once, k8.
Row 11: P8, *K5, [p1, yo, p1] in same st, k5*, p19; rep between *'s once, p8 – 61sts.
Row 12: K8, *p5, k3, p5*, k19; rep between *'s once, k8.
Row 13: P8, *work 5 tog, p in front and back of next st, p1, p in front and back of next st, work 5 tog*, p19; rep between *'s once, p8 – 49 sts.

Center Heart (49 sts)

Row 1 (RS): P24, double inc, p24 – 51 sts.
Rows 2, 4, 6 and 8: K the knit sts and p the purl sts.
Row 3: P22, p2tog, k1, double inc, k1, p2tog, p22.
Row 5: P21, p2tog, k2, double inc, k2, p2tog, p21.
Row 7: P20, p2tog, k3, double inc, k3, p2tog, p20.
Row 9: P21, k4, double inc, k4, p21 – 53 sts.
Row 10: K21, p5, k1, p5, k21.
Row 11: P21, k5, [p1, yo, p1] in same st, k5, p21 – 55 sts.
Row 12: K21, p5, k3, p5, k21.
Row 13: P21, work 5 tog, p in front and back of next st, p1, p in front and back of next st, work 5 tog, p21 – 49 sts.

BLOCK 7

With color E, cont on 61 sts from Block 6 as follows:
Next Row (RS): Work 3 sts in **Garter**, 55 sts in **Bobbles**, 3 sts in Garter. Cont in pats as established until block measures 12½"/32 cm, end with a WS row. Change to color D and k 4 rows, dec 9 sts evenly across first row and inc 6 sts evenly across last row – 58 sts. Cut yarn.

MB = Make Bobble K in front, back, front and back of st, turn, p4, turn, k4, turn, p2tog twice, turn, k2tog.

Bobbles (multiple of 6 sts plus 1)
Rows 1–4: Starting with a k row, work in St st.
Row 5 (RS): K3, *MB, k5; rep from *, end MB, k3.
Rows 6–8: Starting with p row, work in St st.
Row 9 (RS): K6, *MB, k5; rep from *, end MB, k6.
Rep rows 2–9 for Bobbles pat.

BLOCK 8

With color B, cont on 58 sts from Block 7 as follows:
Next Row (RS): Work 3 sts in **Garter**, 52 sts in **Basketweave**, 3 sts in **Garter**. Cont in pats as established until block measures 12½"/32 cm from beg, end with WS row. K 4 rows, dec 6 sts evenly across first row - 52 sts. Bind off knitwise.

Basketweave (multiple of 16 sts plus 4)
Row 1 (RS): *K8, p8; rep from *, end k4.
Rows 2–10: K the knit sts and p the purl sts.
Row 11: *P8, k8; rep from *, end p4.
Rows 12–20: K the knit sts and p the purl sts.
Rep rows 1–20 for Basketweave pat.

STRIP 3

BLOCK 9

With color F, cast on 52 sts. K 4 rows, inc 13 sts evenly across last row – 65 sts. Work in pats as follows: Next Row (RS): Work 3 sts in **Garter**, 59 sts in **Cable Panels**, 3 sts in **Garter**. Cont in pats as established until piece measures 13"/33 cm from beg, end with WS row. Change to color D and k 4 rows, dec 13 sts evenly across first row and inc 9 sts evenly across last row – 61 sts. Cut yarn.

Cable Panels (multiple of 10 sts plus 9)
Row 1 (RS): P2, *k5, p5; rep from *, end k5, p2.
Row 2: K2, *p2, sl 1, p2, k5; rep from *, end last rep k2 instead of k5.
Row 3: P2, *sl 2 wyib, drop next st to front, sl first 2 sts from RH needle back to LH needle, pick up dropped st and knit it, k4, p5; rep from *, end last rep p2 instead of p5.
Row 4: Rep row 2.
Row 5: P2, *k2, drop next st to front, k2, pick up dropped st and knit it, p5; rep from *, end last rep p2 instead of p5.
Rep rows 2–5 for Cable Panels pat.

BLOCK 10

With color C, cont on 61 sts from Block 9 as follows:
Next Row (RS): Work 3 sts in **Garter**, 55 sts in **Squares**, 3 sts in Garter. Cont in pats as established until block measures 12½"/32 cm, end with row 7. P next row. Change to color A and k 4 rows, dec 9 sts evenly across first row and inc 8 sts evenly across last row – 60 sts. Cut yarn.

Squares (multiple of 6 sts plus 1)
Row 1 (RS): Knit.
Row 2 (WS): *P2, k3, p1; rep from *, end p2, k3, p2.
Rows 3 and 4: K the knit sts and p the purl sts.
Row 5 (RS): Rep row 2.
Rows 6 and 7: K the knit sts and p the purl sts.
Rep rows 2–7 for Squares pat.

BLOCK 11

With color D, cont on 60 sts from Block 9 as follows:

Next Row (RS): Work 3 sts in **Garter**, 54 sts in **Double Broken Rib**, 3 sts in **Garter**. Cont in pats as established until block measures 12½"/32 cm, end with a WS row. Change to color F and k 4 rows, dec 8 sts evenly across first row and inc 23 sts across last row – 75 sts. Cut yarn.

Double Broken Rib (multiple of 4 sts plus 2)

Row 1 (RS): Knit.

Row 2: Purl.

Row 3: K2, *p2, k2; rep from *.

Row 4: P2, *k2, p2; rep from *.

Rep rows 1–4 for Double Broken Rib pat.

BLOCK 12

With color A, cont on 75 sts from Block 11 as follows:

Next Row (RS): Work 3 sts in **Garter**, 69 sts in **Diagonal**, 3 sts in **Garter**. Cont in pats as established until block measures 12½"/32 cm, end with a WS row. K 4 rows, dec 23 sts evenly across first row - 52 sts. Bind off knitwise.

Diagonal (multiple of 4 sts plus 1)

Rows 1 and 3 (RS): Knit.

Row 2: *P1, p3tog but do not drop sts from needle, yo, p3 tog again, dropping sts from LH needle; rep from *, end p1.

Row 4: P3, *p3tog but do not drop sts from needle, yo, p3 tog again, dropping sts from LH needle, p1; rep from *, end last rep p3 instead of p1.

Rep rows 1–4 for Diagonal pat.

FINISHING Block each strip to measurements. Sew strips together following placement diagram, and using Seaming Method 2 shown on page 10. **Fringe (optional):** Cut 312 strands 12"/30.5 cm long. With crochet hook, attach 156 strands along cast on edge and 156 strands along bound-off edge as follows: Fold group of 4 strands in half. With RS of blanket facing, insert hook up through edge and pull loop through. Draw ends through loop and tighten. Trim ends.

COLORWAY 2

Tribal

SIZE 50" x 60" / 126 x 152cm

MATERIALS Manos del Uruguay. Knitting needles size 9US / 5.5mm. Circular needle 29" or longer size 8 US / 5mm. Crochet hook H / 4.75mm for fringe.

	Color	Skns		Color	Skns
A.	Cameo 52	3	E.	Cinnamon V	3
B.	Copper 28	3	F.	Uranium 35	3
C.	Briar 44	4	G.	Putty K	3
D.	Silica 30	3			

GAUGE 16 sts and 24 rows = 4" / 10cm in pat sts

NOTE *Throw is made up of 4 identical blocks. Borders are added after blocks are sewn together. Check off rows as you go, and check stitch count frequently. When increasing, you should always have 1 more st on your needle than the row # you just completed; i.e. when you finish row 10, you should have 11 sts on the needle.*

RS inc: K into front and back of st.

WS inc: P into front and back of st.

BLOCK (MAKE 4)

With A, cast on 1 st.

Row 1 (RS): RS inc – 2 sts.

Row 2: K1, WS inc – 3 sts.

Row 3: K2, RS inc – 4 sts.

Row 4: K3, WS inc – 5 sts.

Cont to work rows as indicated, inc 1 in the last st of each row.

Rows 5–14: K.

Row 15: With B, k.

Row 16: P.

Row 17: K.

Rows 18–21: DS.

Row 22: P.

Rows 23–28: With C, k.

Row 29: With D, k.

Row 30: P.

Rows 31–34: K.

Row 35: With E, k.

Row 36: P.

Row 37: K2, *yo, k2 tog; rep from * across.

DS = DOUBLE SEED

Row 1: *P1, k1; rep from * across.

Row 2: K the k sts and p the p sts.

Row 3: P the k sts and k the p sts.

Row 4: Rep row 2.

Repeat rows 2 and 3 for additional rows.

DR = DOUBLE RIB

Row 1: *K2, p2; rep from *.

All other rows: K the k sts and p the p sts.

SR = SINGLE RIB

Row 1: *P1, k1; rep from * across

All other rows: K the k sts and p the p sts.

MB = MAKE BOBBLE

K, p, k, p into the same st. Then, one at a time, pull 2nd, 3rd and 4th sts over first st.

Row 38: K.

Row 39: With C, k.

Row 40: P.

Rows 41 and 42: DR.

Row 43: K.

Row 44: P.

Rows 45–48: With A, k.

Row 49: With E, k.

Rows 50–52: SR.

Rows 53–58: With B, k.

Row 59: With D, k.

Row 60: P.

Row 61: K2, *yo, k2 tog, rep from * across.

Row 62: P.

Rows 63 and 64: K.

Row 65: With C, k.

Rows 66–69: DS.

Row 70: P.

Rows 71–76: With E, k.

Row 77: With A, k.

Row 78: P.

Rows 79–82: K.

Row 83: With B, k.

Row 84: P.

Row 85: K2, *MB, k2; rep from * across.

Row 86: P.

Rows 87–90: With C, k.

Row 91: With D, k.

Rows 92–94: SR.

Rows 95–97: With E, k.

Row 98: P.

Row 99: K2, *yo, k2 tog; rep from * across.

Rows 100–102: K.

Row 103: With B, k.

Rows 104–106: DR.

Row 107: K.

Row 108: P.

Rows 109–113: With C, k.

Row 114: P.

Rows 115–118: With A, k.

Row 119: With F, k.

Row 120: P.

Row 121: K2, *MB, k2; rep from * across.

Row 122: P.

Rows 123 – 127: With D, k.

Row 128: P.

Rows 129 and 130: With E, k.

Rows 131 and 132: SR.

Rows 133–136: K.

*There are now 137 sts on needle. Continue and **dec 1 st** at the end of each row.*

Row 137: With G, k.

Rows 138–141: DR.

Row 142: P.

Rows 143–147: With B, k.

Row 148: P.

Rows 149– 151: With F, k.

Row 152: P.

Row 153: K2, *yo, k2 tog; rep from * across.

Row 154: P.

Rows 155 and 156: K.

Rows 157–161: With D, k.

Row 162: P.

Rows 163–165: K.

Row 166: P.

Rows 167–170: With A, k.

Row 171: With G, k.

Rows 172–175: DS.

Row 176: P.

Rows 177–180: With C, k.

Row 181: With F, k.

Row 182: P.

Row 183: K.

Row 184: P.

Rows 185 and 186: K.

Row 187: With D, k.

Rows 188–191: DR.

Rows 192–194: K.

Row 195: With G, k.

Row 196: P.

Row 197: K3, *MB, k2; rep from * across.

Row 198: P.

Rows 199–202: With A, k.

Row 203: With B, k.

Row 204: P.

Rows 205–207: K.

Row 208: P.

Rows 209–212: K.

Row 213: With F, k.

Rows 214–219: DS.

Row 220: P.

Rows 221–224: With D, k.

Rows 225–227: DR.

Row 228: P.

Rows 229–233: With C, k.

Row 234: P.

Rows 235–239: K.

Row 240: P.

Rows 241–245: K.

Row 246: P.

Rows 247–251: K.

Row 252: P.

With C, k all rem rows, dec 1 st end of each row until 4 sts rem.

Next row: K1, k2 tog, k1.

Next row: K1, k2 tog.

Next row: K2 tog.

Cut yarn and pull end thru loop.

Sew blocks together as indicated in diagram using Seaming Method 1 on page 10.

BORDERS With C and size 9US / 5.5mm needle, right side facing, pick up 200 sts along top edge of throw. In Garter st, work stripes as follows: 3 rows C, 4 rows G, 4 rows F, 2 rows B, 4 rows G, 2 rows B, 4 rows F, 4 rows G, 4 rows C, 4 rows G, 3 rows C. Bind off. Repeat border along bottom edge.

FINISHING With size 8 US / 5mm circular needle and C, right side facing, pick up approx. 240 sts along side edge. K 3 rows. Bind off. Repeat along other side.

FRINGE Make 50 twisted fringes along each short end as follows: For each twist, cut 3 pieces of color E, each 16" / 40mm long. Fold in half. With right side of throw facing, push crochet hook up through edge, pull loop of fringe through, pull ends of fringe through loop. Take 3 ends in your right hand between your thumb and index fingers; take 3 ends in your left hand, also between your thumb and index fingers. Twist each group several times to the right until both twists are tight. While keeping twists tight, twist both groups together to the left. Secure with an overhand knot at the bottom. Trim ends.

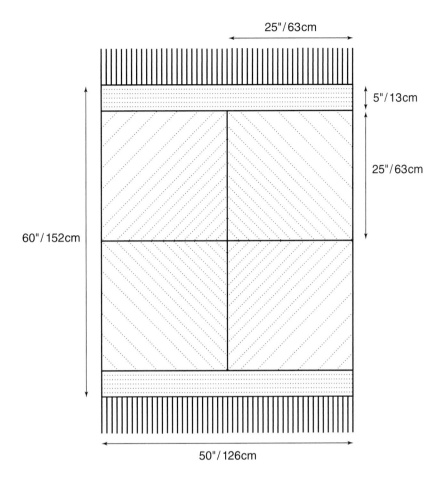

25"/63cm

5"/13cm

25"/63cm

60"/152cm

50"/126cm

TRIBAL PILLOW

SIZE 18" x 18" / 45 x 45cm

MATERIALS Manos del Uruguay. Small amounts of 7 colors as used in Tribal Throw. Knitting needles size 9US / 5.5mm.

PILLOW Work 2 blocks as for Tribal Throw, page 29, working rows 1–91. Side edge should measure 18" / 45cm; diagonal measurement from point to needle should be approx. 12¾" / 32cm. Cont to work rows 92–182, dec 1 st at the end of each row.

FINISHING Sew 3 sides of pillow together so that lines of pats match at seams. With E and RS facing, pick up 70 sts along one rem edge. K 3 rows. **Next row (RS):** K1, *yo, k2 tog; rep from *, end k1. K 3 rows. Bind off. Rep along rem edge.

Rope: Cut 6 36" / 90cm long pieces of yarn in varied colors. Tie together with overhand knot. Attach tied end to something stationary and twist into a rope following directions on page 30 for fringe. Secure end with an overhand knot. Make pillow lining following directions on page 60 and insert. Overlap edges of pillow cover and weave rope through eyelets as follows: Pull end of rope down through first hole of both edges; pull rope through, leaving about 6" / 15cm hanging. *Pass long end up through the next hole of the lower edge, then up through the next hole of the upper edge. Pass end down through the next hole of the upper edge and down through the next hole of the lower edge. Rep from * across, pulling rope snugly so edges overlap. To remove pillow liner for cleaning, slide out rope by untying knot at one end.

eSg

SIZE 39" x 52" / 99 x 132cm

MATERIALS Manos del Uruguay. 1 skein for each block and 1 skein for fringe. Needles size 9US / 5.5mm *or size needed to obtain gauge.* Crochet hook H / 4.75mm for fringe.

GAUGE 16 sts = 4" / 10cm in pat sts

Block	Colorway 1 (p.32)	Colorway 2 (p.35)
1	Steel 29	Thrush 37
2	Cirrus 39	Rust U
3	Cornflower 62	Cinnamon V
4	Lapis 45	Thistle 41
5	Thistle 41	Coffee G
6	French Blue 60	Bing Cherry M
7	Raspberry 57	Topaz X
8	Mallard 36	Olive 55
9	Petrol 27	Uranium 35
10	Heather 50	Brick 54
11	Juniper 43	Briar 44
12	Aster 38	Cinnamon V

39"/99cm

13"/33cm

13"/33cm

52"/132cm

Block 12	Block 8	Block 4
Block 11	Block 7	Block 3
Block 10	Block 6	Block 2
Block 9	Block 5	Block 1

Strip 3 · Strip 2 · Strip 1

STRIP 1

BLOCK 1

Cast on 52 sts. K 4 rows, inc 4 sts evenly on last row – 56 sts. Work pats as follows: **Next Row (RS):** Work 3 sts in **Garter**, 50 sts in **Double Moss**, 3 sts in **Garter**. Cont in pats as established until block measures 12¾" /32.5 cm from beg, end with WS row. K 2 rows, dec 4 sts evenly on first row – 52 sts. Cut yarn.

Double Moss (multiple of 4 sts plus 2)
Row 1 (RS): *K2, p2; rep from *, end k2.
Rows 2 and 4: K the knit sts and p the purl sts.
Row 3: *P2, k2; rep from *, end p2.
Rep rows 1–4 for Double Moss pat.

BLOCK 2

With new color, cont on 52 sts from Block 1 as follows: K 2 rows, inc 8 sts evenly across last row – 60 sts. Work pats as follows: **Next row (RS):** Work 3 sts in **Garter**, 54 sts in **Beaded Rib**, 3 sts in **Garter**. Cont in pats as established until block measures 12¾"/ 32.5 cm from beg, end with a WS row. K 2 rows, dec 8 sts evenly across first row – 52 sts. Cut yarn.

Beaded Rib (over any number of sts)
Row 1 (RS): *K1, p1; rep from * to end.
Row 2: Knit.
Rep rows 1 and 2 for Beaded Rib pat.

BLOCK 3

With new color, cont working on 52 sts from Block 2 as follows: K 2 rows, inc 10 sts evenly across last row – 62 sts. Work pats as follows: **Next Row (RS):** Work 3 sts **Garter**, p2, work 14 sts **Staghorn Cable #1**, p2, k1, p2, work 14 sts **Staghorn Cable #2**, p2, k1, p2, work 14 sts **Staghorn Cable #1**, p2, work 3 sts **Garter**. Cont in pats as established, working sts outside of cables as k the knit sts and p the purl sts, until block measures 12¾"/32.5 cm from beg, end with a WS row. K 2 rows, dec 10 sts evenly across first row – 52 sts. Cut yarn.

Staghorn Cable #1 (over 14 sts)
C3L = sl 2 sts to cn and hold to front of work, k1, k2 from cn.
C3R = sl 1 st to cn and hold to back of work, k2, k1 from cn.
Row 1 (RS): C3L, k1, C3L, C3R, k1, C3R.
Rows 2, 4, 6 and 8: Purl.
Row 3: K1, C3L, k6, C3R, k1.
Row 5: K2, C3L, k4, C3R, k2.
Row 7: K3, C3L, k2, C3R, k3.
Rep rows 1–8 for Staghorn Cable #1 pat.

Staghorn Cable #2 (over 14 sts)
Row 1 (RS): C3R, k1, C3R, C3L, k1, C3L.
Rows 2, 4, 6 and 8: Purl.
Row 3: K3, C3R, k2, C3L, k3.
Row 5: K2, C3R, k4, C3L, k2.
Row 7: K1, C3R, k6, C3L, k1.
Rep rows 1–8 for Staghorn Cable #2 pat.

BLOCK 4

With new color, cont on 52 sts from Block 3 as follows: K 2 rows. Work pats as follows: **Next Row (RS):** Work 3 sts in **Garter**, 46 sts in **St st/Garter Rib**, 3 sts in **Garter**. Cont in pats as established until block measures 12½" /31.5 cm from beg, end with a WS row. K 4 rows. Bind off knitwise.

St st /Garter Rib (multiple of 6 sts plus 4)
Row 1 (RS): Knit.
Row 2: *P4, k2; rep from *, end p4.
Rep rows 1 and 2 for St st/Garter Rib pat.

COLORWAY 2

STRIP 2

BLOCK 5

With new color, cast on 52 sts. K 4 rows, inc 10 sts evenly across last row – 62 sts. Cont in pats as follows: **Next Row (RS)**: Work 3 sts in **Garter**, 8 sts in **St st**, 16 sts **Cable Panel**, 8 sts in **St st**, 16 sts **Cable Panel**, 8 sts in **St st**, 3 sts **Garter**. Cont in pats as established until block measures 12¾"/32.5 cm from beg, end with a WS row. K 2 rows, dec 10 sts evenly across first row – 52 sts. Cut yarn.

Cable Panel (over 16 sts)

Rows 1, 3, 5 and 7 (RS): [P1, k1] twice, p1, k6, [p1, k1] twice, p1.

Rows 2, 4, 6, 8 and 10: K the knit sts and p the purl sts.

Row 9: [P1, k1] twice, p1, sl 3 sts to cn and hold to back of work, k3, k3 from cn, [p1, k1] twice, p1.

Repeat rows 1–10 for Cable Panel pat.

BLOCK 6

With new color, cont on 52 sts from Block 5 as follows: K 2 rows, inc 3 sts evenly across last row – 55 sts. Cont in pats as follows: Work first and last 3 sts in garter st and rem sts in St st for 8 rows. Work **Diamond Motif** as follows: **Next 2 rows:** Work 3 sts **Garter**, 24 sts **St st**, 1 st **Garter**, 24 sts **St st**, 3 sts **Garter**. **Next 2 rows:** Work 3 sts **Garter**, 23 sts **St st**, 3 sts **Garter**, 23 sts **St st**, 3 sts **Garter**. **Next 2 rows:** Work 3 sts **Garter**, 22 sts **St st**, 5 sts **Garter**, 22 sts **St st**, 3 sts **Garter**. Cont in this way to work 2 more center sts in Garter st every other row until there are 29 center sts in Garter. Cont by working 2 fewer Garter sts in center every other row until there is 1 Garter st in center. Work first and last 3 sts in garter st and rem sts in St st for 12 rows or until block measures 12¾"/32.5 cm from beg, end with a WS row. K 2 rows, dec 3 sts evenly across first row – 52 sts. Cut yarn.

BLOCK 7

With new color, cont working on 52 sts from Block 6 as follows: K 2 rows, inc 10 sts evenly across last row – 62 sts. Work pats as follows: **Next row (RS)**: Work 3 sts in **Garter** , 56 sts in **Mistake St Ribbing**, 3 sts in **Garter**. Cont in pats as established until block measures 12¾"/ 32.5 cm from beg, end with a WS row. K 2 rows, dec 10 sts evenly across first row – 52 sts. Cut yarn.

Mistake Stitch Ribbing (multiple of 4 sts)

Row 1 (RS): *K1, P2, K1; rep from * to end.

Row 2: *P2, K2; rep from * to end.

Rep rows 1 and 2 for Mistake St Ribbing pat.

BLOCK 8

With new color, cont working on 52 sts from Block 7 as follows: K 2 rows, inc 2 sts evenly across last row – 54 sts. Work pats as follows: **Next row (RS)**: Work 3 sts in **Garter**, 48 sts in **Seed St**, 3 sts in **Garter**. Cont in pats as established until block measures 12½"/ 31.5 cm from beg, end with a WS row. K 4 rows, dec 2 sts evenly across first row – 52 sts. Bind off knitwise.

Seed Stitch (over an even number of sts)

Row 1 (RS): *K1, p1; rep from * to end.

Row 2: *P1, k1; rep from * to end.

Rep rows 1 and 2 for Seed St pat.

STRIP 3

BLOCK 9

With new color, cast on 52 sts. K 4 rows, inc 6 sts evenly across last row – 58 sts. Work pats as follows: **Next row (RS):** Work 3 sts in **Garter**, 52 sts in **Basketweave**, 3 sts in **Garter**. Cont in pats as established until block measures 12¾"/ 32.5 cm from beg, end with a WS row. K 2 rows, dec 6 sts evenly across first row – 52 sts. Cut yarn.

Basketweave (multiple of 8 sts plus 4)
Rows 1 and 3 (RS): *K4, p4; rep from *, end k4.
Rows 2, 4, 6, and 8: K the knit sts and p the purl sts.
Rows 5 and 7: *P4, k4; rep from *, end p4.
Rep rows 1–8 for Basketweave pat.

BLOCK 10

With new color, cont on 52 sts from Block 9 as follows: K 2 rows, inc 2 sts evenly across last row – 54 sts. Work pats as follows: **Next row (RS):** Work 3 sts in **Garter**, 48 sts in **Moss**, 3 sts in **Garter**. Cont in pats as established until block measures 12¾"/ 32.5 cm from beg, end with a WS row. K 2 rows, dec 2 sts evenly across first row – 52 sts. Cut yarn.

Moss Stitch (over an even number of sts)
Rows 1 and 2 (RS): *K1, p1; rep from * to end.
Rows 3 and 4: *P1, k1; rep from * to end.
Rep rows 1–4 for Moss St pat.

BLOCK 11

With new color, cont on 52 sts from Block 10 as follows: K 2 rows, inc 10 sts evenly across last row – 62 sts. Work pats as follows: **Next row (RS):** Work 3 sts in **Garter**, [5 sts in **St st**, 12 sts **Horseshoe Cable**] 3 times, 5 sts in **St st**, 3 sts **Garter**. Cont in pats as established until block measures 12¾"/ 32.5 cm from beg, end with a WS row. K 2 rows, dec 10 sts evenly across first row – 52 sts. Cut yarn.

Horseshoe Cable (over 12 sts)
Rows 1, 3, 5 and 9 (RS): *P2, k8, p2.
Rows 2, 4, 6, 8, and 10: *K2, p8, k2.
Row 7: P2, sl 2 sts to cn and hold to back, k2, k2 from cn, sl 2 sts to cn and hold to front, k2, k2 from cn, p2.
Rep rows 1–10 for Horseshoe Cable pat.

BLOCK 12

With new color, cont on 52 sts from Block 11 as follows: K 2 rows, inc 2 sts evenly across last row – 54 sts. Work pats as follows: **Next row (RS):** Work 3 sts in **Garter**, 48 sts in **Basket**, 3 sts **Garter**. Cont in pats as established until block measures 12½"/ 31.5 cm from beg, end with a WS row. K 4 rows, dec 2 sts evenly across first row – 52 sts. Bind off knitwise.

Basket Stitch (multiple of 8 sts)
Rows 1, 3, 5 and 7 (RS): Knit.
Rows 2 and 4: *K4, p4; rep from * to end.
Rows 6 and 8: *P4, k4; rep from * to end.
Rep rows 1–8 for Basket Stitch pat.

FINISHING Block each strip to measurements. Following placement diagram, sew strips together using Seaming Method 2 on page 10. **Fringe:** Cut 312 strands 12"/30.5 cm long. With crochet hook, attach 156 strands along cast-on edge and 156 strands along bound-off edge as follows: Fold group of 4 strands in half. With RS of blanket facing, insert hook up through edge and pull loop through. Draw ends through loop and tighten. Trim ends.

AMISH

Directions page 40

Directions page 42

Amish

Pictured page 38

SIZE 44" x 44" / 110 x 110cm

MATERIALS Manos del Uruguay. Knitting needles size 9US / 5.5mm *or size needed to achieve gauge.* Crochet hook G / 4.25mm.

	Color	skns		Color	skns
A.	Black 08	5	E.	Bing Cherry M	1
B.	Raspberry 57	2	F.	Mallard 36	1
C.	Heliotrope 63	1	G.	Aster 38	1
D.	Olive 55	1			

GAUGE 16 sts = 4" / 10cm in pat sts

STRIP 1

With C, cast on 26 sts.

Row 1 (WS): P1, *k1, p1; rep from *, end k1, p2.

Row 2: K.

Repeat rows 1 and 2 until piece measures 30" / 75cm, end row 1. Bind off knitwise.

STRIP 2

With D, cast on 26 sts.

Rows 1 and 5 (WS): P.

Rows 2 and 6: K.

Row 3: P2, *k2, p2; rep from *.

Row 4: K2, *p2, k2; rep from *.

Row 7: P1, k1, *p2, k2; rep from *, end p2, k1, p1.

Row 8: K1, p1, *k2, p2; rep from *, end k2, p1, k1.

Repeat rows 1–8 until piece measures 30" / 75cm, end with a WS row. Bind off knitwise.

STRIP 3

With E, cast on 26 sts.

Rows 1 and 3 (WS): P1, *k4, p4; rep from *, end k4, p5.

Rows 2 and 4: K5; *p4, k4; rep from *, end p4, k1.

Rows 5 and 7: P5, *k4, p4; rep from *, end k4, p1.

Rows 6 and 8: K1, *p4, k4; rep from *, end p4, k5.

Repeat rows 1–8 until piece measures 30" / 75cm, end with a WS row. Bind off knitwise.

STRIP 4

With F, cast on 26 sts.

Row 1 (WS): P1, *k1, p1; rep from *, end k1, p2.

Row 2: K1, *p3, k3; rep from *, end p3, k4.

Repeat rows 1 and 2 until piece measures 30 / 75cm", end with a WS row. Bind off knitwise.

STRIP 5

With G, cast on 26 sts.

Row 1 (WS): P1, *k1, p1; rep from *, end k1, p2.

Row 2: K1, *p1, k1; rep from *, end p1, k2.

Repeat rows 1 and 2 until piece measures 30" / 75cm, end with a WS row. Bind off knitwise.

NOTE All patterns include 1 st at each edge for seaming. Using Seaming Method 1 on page 10, sew strips together per diagram. Measure the width of this section = *Width A.*

CORNERS (make 4)

Bobble = K into the front, then back, then front, then back of the same st. Turn, p4, Turn, k4 tog.

With B, cast on 30 sts. K 5 rows.

Rows 1 and 5 (RS): K.

Rows 2, 4 and 6 (WS): P1, k4, p20, k4, p1.

Rows 3: K7, (**Bobble**, k4) 3 times, **Bobble**, k7.

Repeat rows 3–6 until piece measures 6¼" / 16cm, end row 5. K 5 rows. Bind off. Piece should measure 7" / 18cm square.

BORDERS (make 4)

With A, cast on 30 sts.

Row 1 (WS): P5, *k4, p4; rep from *, end k4, p5.

Row 2: K1, P4, *k4, p4; rep from *, end k1.

Borders 1 and 2: Repeat rows 1 and 2 until piece measures 30" / 75cm, end row 1. Bind off knitwise.

Borders 3 and 4: Repeat rows 1 and 2 until piece measures the same as *Width A*.

FINISHING

Sew remaining pieces together. With A and crochet hook, work **Shrimp St** around entire edge.

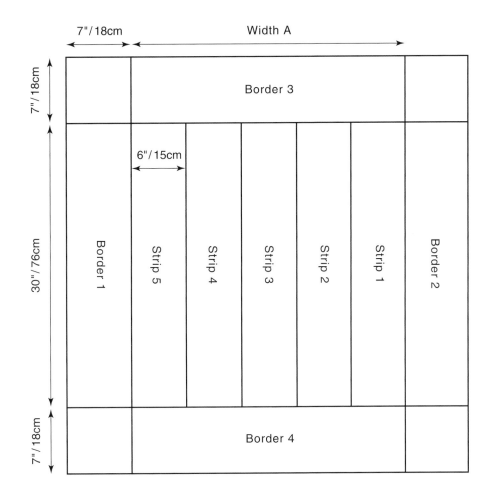

Seascape

Pictured page 39

SIZE 40" x 50" / 100 x 125cm

MATERIALS Manos Del Uruguay. Knitting needles size 9US / 5.5mm *or size to obtain given gauge.*

	Color	skns		Color	skns
A.	Navy 11	2	D.	Powder C	4
B.	Cornflower 62	5	E.	Midnight A	1
C.	Lapis 45	1		Fringe: 1 skein A	

GAUGE 16 sts = 4" / 10 cm in pat sts.

BLOCK 1
K all rows for 4" / 10cm, end WS row.

BLOCK 2
Row 1 (WS): [P2, k2] 7 times, p2, k4.
Row 2: K6, [p2, k2] 7 times.
Row 3: [K2, p2] 7 times, k6.
Row 4: K4, [p2, k2] 7 times, p2.
Repeat rows 1–4.

BLOCK 3
Row 1 (WS): K4, [p2, k2] 7 times, p2.
Row 2: [K2, p2] 7 times, k6.
Row 3: K6, [p2, k2] 7 times.
Row 4: [P2, k2] 7 times, p2, k4.
Repeat rows 1–4.

BLOCK 4
Row 1 (WS): [K2, p2] 8 times, k2.
Rows 2 and 4: K the k sts and p the p sts.
Row 3: [P2, k2] 8 times, p2.
Repeat rows 1–4.

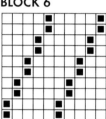

BLOCK 5   **BLOCK 6**

Row 1: WS.
Read WS rows from left to right and RS rows from right to left.

■ = p on RS, k on WS
□ = k on RS, p on WS

STRIP 1 With A, cast on 34 sts. *Work Block 1. Cut yarn. **Next row (RS):** With B, k. Work Block 2 for 19" / 48cm, end RS row. **Next row (WS):** P row, keeping edge sts k4. Cut yarn.* With C, k. Rep from * to *. With A, work Block 1. Bind off.

STRIP 2 With D, cast on 34 sts. Work Block 1 for 2". **Next row (RS):** K. Work Block 5 for 9½" / 25cm, end RS row. *Mark last row worked on chart. P next row. Cut yarn. With E, work Block 1. Cut yarn. With D, k.* Cont to work Block 5 for 19" / 48cm, starting with next row in pat. End RS row. Rep from * to *. Cont to work Block 5 for 9½" / 25cm, end RS row. Work Block 1 for 2", end WS. Bind off knitwise.

STRIP 3 Work as for Strip 1, substituting Block 4 for Block 2.

STRIP 4 Work as for Strip 2, substituting Block 6 for Block 5.

STRIP 5 Work as for Strip 1, substituting Block 3 for Block 2.

FINISHING Sew strips together using Seaming Method 1 on page 10.

FRINGE Cut 270 strands 16"/40cm long. With crochet hook, attach 135 strands along cast-on edge and 135 strands along bound-off edge as follows: Fold group of 3 strands in half. With RS of blanket facing, insert hook up through edge and pull loop through. Draw ends through loop and tighten. Trim ends.

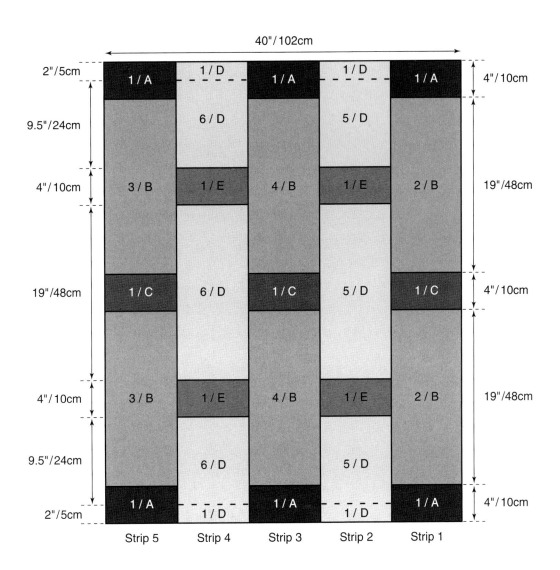

Baby Blocks

SIZE 35" x 36" / 88 x 90cm

MATERIALS Manos del Uruguay: 3 skns color **A.** Butane 33; 2 skns each, colors **B.** Mint 18, **C.** Heather 50, **D.** Parma 20; 1 skn **E.** Mist 22. Knitting needles size 9US / 5.5mm *or size needed to obtain gauge.* Crochet hook H / 4.75mm

GAUGE

16 sts and 24 rows = 4" / 10cm in pat sts

STRIPS 1 AND 7

1. With A, cast on 24 sts. K 3 rows. Work Block I. K 3 rows.
2. With A, k 4 rows. Work Block I. K 3 rows.
3. With B, k 3 rows. **Next row (WS):** K, dec 1 st – 23 sts. Work Block II. **Next row (WS):** K, inc 1 st – 24 sts. K 2 rows.
4. With C, k 3 rows. **Next row (WS):** K, dec 3 sts evenly across – 21 sts. Work Block III. **Next row (WS):** K, inc 3 sts evenly across – 24 sts. K 2 rows.
5. With B, k 3 rows. **Next row (WS):** K, dec 1 st – 23 sts. Work Block II. **Next row (WS):** K, inc 1 st – 24 sts. K 2 rows.
6. With A, k 4 rows. Work Block I. K 3 rows.
7. With A, k 4 rows. Work Block I. K 3 rows. Bind off knitwise.

STRIPS 2 AND 6

1. With A, cast on 24 sts. K 3 rows. Work Block I. K 3 rows.
2. With B, k 3 rows. **Next row (WS):** K, dec 1 st – 23 sts. Work Block II. **Next row (WS):** K, inc 1 st – 24 sts. K 2 rows.
3. With C, k 3 rows. **Next row (WS):** K, dec 3 sts evenly across – 21 sts. Work Block III. **Next row (WS):** K, inc 3 sts evenly across – 24 sts. K 2 rows.
4. With D, k 3 rows. **Next row (WS):** K, dec 1 st – 23 sts. Work Block IV. **Next row (WS):** K, inc 1 st – 24 sts. K 2 rows.
5. With C, k 3 rows. **Next row (WS):** K, dec 3 sts evenly across – 21 sts. Work Block III. **Next row (WS):** K, inc 3 sts evenly across – 24 sts. K 2 rows.
6. With B, k 3 rows. **Next row (WS):** K, dec 1 st – 23 sts. Work Block II. **Next row (WS):** K, inc 1 st – 24 sts. K 2 rows.

7. With A, k 4 rows. Work Block I. K 3 rows. Bind off knitwise.

STRIPS 3 AND 5

1. With B, cast on 24 sts. K 2 rows. **Next row (WS):** K, dec 1 st – 23 sts. Work Block II. **Next row (WS):** K, inc 1 st – 24 sts. K 2 rows.
2. With C, k 3 rows. **Next row (WS):** K, dec 3 sts evenly across – 21 sts. Work Block III. **Next row (WS):** K, inc 3 sts evenly across – 24 sts. K 2 rows.
3. With D, k 3 rows. **Next row (WS):** K, dec 1 st – 23 sts. Work Block IV. **Next row (WS):** K, inc 1 st – 24 sts. K 2 rows.
4. With E, k 4 rows. Work Block V. K 3 rows.
5. With D, k 3 rows. **Next row (WS):** K, dec 1 st – 23 sts. Work Block IV. **Next row (WS):** K, inc 1 st – 24 sts. K 2 rows.
6. With C, k 3 rows. **Next row (WS):** K, dec 3 sts evenly across – 21 sts. Work Block III. **Next row (WS):** K, inc 3 sts evenly across – 24 sts. K 2 rows.
7. With B, k 3 rows. **Next row (WS):** K, dec 1 st – 23 sts. Work Block II. **Next row (WS):** K, inc 1 st – 24 sts. K 2 rows. Bind off knitwise.

STRIP 4

1 With C, cast on 24 sts. K 2 rows. **Next row (WS):** K, dec 3 sts evenly across – 21 sts. Work Block III. **Next row (WS):** K, inc 3 sts evenly across – 24 sts. K 2 rows.
2. With D, k 3 rows. **Next row (WS):** K, dec 1 st – 23 sts. Work Block IV. **Next row (WS):** K, inc 1 st – 24 sts. K 2 rows.
3. With E, k 4 rows. Work Block V. K 3 rows.
4. With A, k 3 rows. **Next row (WS):** K, dec 1 st – 23 sts. Work Center Block. **Next row (WS):** K, inc 1 st – 24 sts. K 2 rows.
5. With E, k 4 rows. Work Block V. K 3 rows.
6. With D, k 3 rows. **Next row (WS):** K, dec 1 st – 23 sts. Work Block IV. **Next row (WS):** K, inc 1 st – 24 sts. K 2 rows.
7. With C, k 3 rows. **Next row (WS):** K, dec 3 sts evenly across – 21 sts. Work Block III. **Next row (WS):** K, inc 3 sts evenly across – 24 sts. K 2 rows. Bind off knitwise.

FINISHING Sew strips together following diagram. Use Seaming Method 2 shown on page 10.

Edging: **Row 1:** With A and crochet hook, work row of sc around entire edge, working 3 sc into each corner.

Row 2: *Sc, ch 1, sk next sc, sc into next st; rep from * around working 1 sc into each of 3 corner single crochets. Sl st to first sc. Cut yarn, and pull end through loop.

BLOCK I (24 sts) Color A

Row 1 (RS): K2, [RT, k4] 3 times, RT, k2.

Row 2 and all WS rows: K2, p20. k2.

Row 3: K3, [LT, k2, RT] 3 times, k3.

Row 5: K4, [LT, RT, k2] 3 times, k2.

Row 7: K5, [RT, k4] 3 times, k1.

Row 9: K4, [RT, LT, k2] 3 times, k2.

Row 11: K3, [RT, k2, LT] 3 times, k3.

Row 12: K2, p20, k2.

Rep rows 1–12 once more, then work row 1.

BLOCK III (21 sts) Color C

Row 1 (RS): K3, [p3, k1] 4 times, k2.

Rows 2 and 4: K2, p17, k2.

Row 3: K2, p2, [k1, p3] 3 times, k1, p2, k2.

Repeat rows 1–4 6 times, then work row 1 again.

BLOCK IV (23 sts) Color D

Row 1 (RS): K8, p1, k5, p1, k8.

Row 2: K3, [p5, k1] twice, p 5, k3.

Row 3: K3, [yo, ssk, p1, k2 tog, yo, k1] 3 times, k2.

Row 4: K3, p2, [k1, p5] twice, k1, p2, k3.

Row 5: K5, [p1, k5] twice, p1, k5.

Row 6: Repeat row 4.

Row 7: K3, [k2 tog, yo, k1, yo, ssk, p1] twice, k2 tog, yo, k1, yo, ssk, k3.

Row 8: Repeat row 2.

Work rows 1–8 a total of 3 times, then work row 1.

BLOCK II (23 sts) Color B

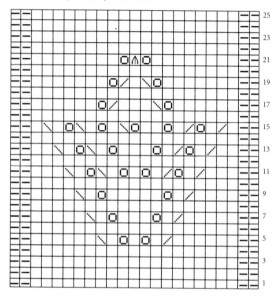

BLOCK V (24 sts) Color E

CENTER BLOCK (23 sts) Color A

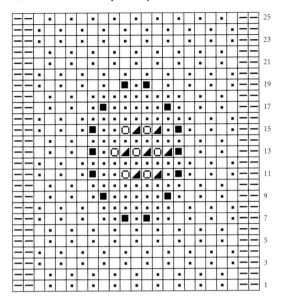

☐ = yo

☐ = K on RS rows, P on WS rows.

▪ = P on RS rows, K on WS rows.

— = K on all rows.

⋀ = Slip 2 sts *as if to* k2 tog, k1, pass both sl sts over.

╱ = K2 tog

╲ = SSK

◢ = P2 tog

■ = Bobble. (K1, p1, k1, p1, k1) into same st, turn, p5, turn. Pass 2nd, 3rd, 4th, 5th sts one at a time over first st then k in back of this st.

36"/90cm

36"/90cm

I	I	II	III	II	I	I
I	II	III	IV	III	II	I
II	III	IV	V	IV	III	II
III	IV	V	center	V	IV	III
II	III	IV	V	IV	III	II
I	II	III	IV	III	II	I
I	I	II	III	II	I	I

Strip 1 2 3 4 5 6 7

· 47 ·

Wildflowers Baby Throw

KNITTED VERSION

SIZE 36" x 36" / 90 x 90cm

MATERIALS Manos Del Uruguay . 29" circular needle size 10US / 6mm *or size needed to obtain gauge.*

	Color	skns		Color	skns
A.	Cornflower 62	2	E.	Butane 33	1
B.	Souffle 21	1	F.	Hollywood 01	1
C.	Rose O	1	G.	Powder C	1
D.	Parma 20	1			

GAUGE 14 sts and 20 rows = 4" / 10cm in garter st

NOTE *Work stitches a little loosely; it will make working the pattern stitch easier. Leave approx. 3" ends for weaving in. Tie the 2 ends of each color together to secure edge.*

COLOR SEQUENCE

A, E, B, * C, D, A, F, G, B, E; rep from *.

THROW

With color A, cast on 121 sts. Knit 6 rows.

Row 1 (WS): With next color, k5, p111, k5.

Row 2: With same color, k7, *yo, k3, pass first of the 3 knit sts over the 2nd and 3rd sts, rep from *, end k6.

Row 3: With next color, k5, p111, k5.

Row 4: With same color, k6, *k3, pass first of the 3 knit sts over the 2nd and 3rd sts, yo; rep from *, end k7.

Repeat rows 1–4 working color sequence for desired length or until one color runs out. With A, k5, p111, k5. K 6 rows. Bind off. Weave ends into border on WS.

CROCHETED VERSION

SIZE 34" x 34" / 85 x 85cm

MATERIALS Manos Del Uruguay. Crochet hook J / 6mm. 2 skns each **A.** Cornflower 62, **B.** Butane 33, **C.** Parma 20.

GAUGE 3 dc = 1" / 2.5cm

PICOT = 1sc, 3ch, sl st to first ch of ch-3.

With A, 5ch, join with sl st to first ch to form ring.

Rnd 1: 5ch (count as 1dc and 2ch), [3dc into ring, 2ch] 3 times, 2dc into ring, sl st to 3rd ch of ch-5.

Rnd 2: With B, sl st into next sp, 5ch, 3dc into same sp, [1ch, 3dc, 2ch, 3dc into next sp] 3 times, 1ch, 2dc into same sp as ch-5 at beg of rnd, sl st to 3rd ch of ch-5.

Rnd 3: With C, sl st into next sp, 5ch, 3dc into same sp, *1ch, 3dc into each sp to corner, [3dc, 2ch, 3dc] into corner; rep from * around, end 2dc into same sp as ch-5.

Rep rnd 3, working colors in sequence as established, for a total of 27 rnds.

EDGING Rnd 1: With A, sl st to corner sp, [1ch, 2sc] into corner sp, *[1sc in each dc, 1sc into each ch-1 sp] to corner, 3sc into corner; rep from * around, end sl st to first ch-1.

Rnd 2: Work **Picot** in each of 3 corner single crochets, *[4sc, **Picot**] to corner, 3 **Picot** in each of 3 corner single crochets; rep from * around, end sl st to first sc. Cut yarn, pull end through loop. Block following washing directions on page 10.

Building Blocks

SIZE 40" x 50" / 100 x 125cm

MATERIALS Manos del Uruguay. Knitting needles
size 9US / 5.5mm *or size needed to obtain gauge.*

	Color	skns
A.	Cherry 48	3
B.	French Blue 60	4
C.	Straw Z	3
D.	Aster 38	2
E.	Malachite 46	2

FLOPPY PILLOW Approx 50 yds each color. To make pillow and throw, add 1 skn each colors C and D to above amounts. Washable stuffing material.

GAUGE

16 sts and 24 rows = 4" / 10cm in pat sts

STRIPS 1 AND 5

1. With A, cast on 40 sts. K 3 rows. Work Block I. K 4 rows.
2. With B, k 3 rows. **Next row (WS):** K7, (inc in next st, k4) 5 times, inc in next st, k7 – 46 sts. Work Block II.
   Next row (RS): K8, (k2 tog, k5) 4 times, k2 tog, k8 – 41 sts. K 3 more rows.
3. With C, k 4 rows. Work Block III. K 4 rows.
4. With B, k 3 rows. **Next row (WS):** K8, (inc in next st, k5) 4 times, inc in next st, k8 – 46 sts. Work Block II.
   Next row (RS): K7, (k2 tog, k4) 5 times, k2 tog, k7 – 40 sts. K 3 more rows.
5. With A, k 4 rows. Work Block I. K 3 rows. Bind off.

STRIPS 2 AND 4

1. With D, cast on 20 sts. K 3 rows. **Next row (RS):** K5, inc in next 3 sts, k4, inc in next 3 sts, k5 – 26 sts. Work Block IV. (**NOTE:** For Strip 2, work cable left; for Strip 4, work cable right.) **Next row (WS):** K5, (k2 tog) 3 times, k4, (k2 tog) 3 times, k5 – 20 sts. K 2 more rows.
2. With E, work Block V.
3. With D, k 2 rows. **Next row (RS):** K5, inc in next 3 sts, k4, inc in next 3 sts, k5 – 26 sts. Work Block IV.
   Next row (WS): K5, (k2 tog) 3 times, k4, (k2 tog) 3 times, k5 – 20 sts. K 2 more rows.
4. With E, work Block V.
5. With D, k 2 rows. **Next row (RS):** K5, inc in next 3 sts, k4, inc in next 3 sts, k5 – 26 sts. Work Block IV.
   Next row (WS): K5, (k2 tog) 3 times, k4, (k2 tog) 3 times, k5 – 20 sts. K 2 more rows. Bind off.

STRIP 3

1. With C, cast on 41 sts. K 3 rows. Work Block III. K 4 rows.
2. With B, knit 3 rows. **Next row (WS):** K8, (inc in next st, k5) 4 times, inc in next st, k8 – 46 sts. Work Block II.
   Next row (RS): K8, (k2 tog, k5) 4 times, k2 tog, k8 – 41 sts. K 3 more rows.
3. With C, k 4 rows. Work Block III. K 4 rows.
4. With B, knit 3 rows. **Next row (WS):** K8, (inc in next st, k5) 4 times, inc in next st, k8 – 46 sts. Work Block II.
   Next row (RS): K8, (k2 tog, k5) 4 times, k2 tog, k8 – 41 sts. K 3 more rows.
5. With C, k 4 rows. Work Block III. K 3 rows. Bind off.

FINISHING Sew strips together, using Seaming Method 2 shown on page 10.

BLOCK I (40 sts)

Row 1 and all RS rows: Knit

Rows 2, 4 and 6: K6, (p4, k4) 3 times, p4, k6.

Rows 8, 10 and 12: K2, p4, (k4, p4) 4 times, k2.

Repeat rows 1–12 a total of 5 times.

BLOCK II (46 sts)

FC = Front Cross: Sl 2 sts to dpn and hold in front, p1, k2 from dpn.

BC = Back Cross: Sl 1 sts to dpn and hold in back, k2, p1 from dpn.

Row 1 (RS): K6, p7 (BC, p4) 3 times, BC, p3, k6.

Rows 2 and all WS rows: K6, K the K sts and P the P sts to the last 6 sts, k6.

Row 3: K6, p6, (BC, p4) 3 times, BC, p4, k6.

Row 5: K6, p5 (BC, p4) 3 times, BC, p5, k6.

Row 7: K6, p4, (BC, p4) 3 times, BC, p6, k6.

Row 9: K6, p3, (BC, p4) 3 times, BC, p7, k6.

Row 11: K6, p3, (FC, p4) 3 times, FC, p7, k6.

Row 13: K6, p4, (FC, p4) 3 times, FC, p6, k6.

Row 15: K6, p5, (FC, p4) 3 times, FC, p5, k6.

Row 17: K6, p6 (FC, p4) 3 times, FC, p4.

Row 19: K6, p7, (FC, p4) 3 times, FC, p3, k6.

Row 20: Rep row 2.

Repeat rows 1–20 a total of 3 times.

BLOCK III (41 sts)

Work chart starting with a RS row.

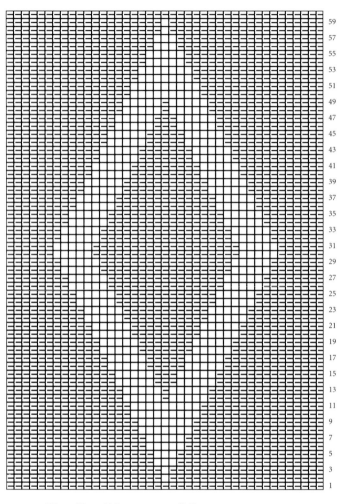

☐ = K on RS rows, p on WS rows

— = K on all rows

BLOCK IV (26 sts)

C6R = Cable Right: Sl 3 sts to dpn and hold in back, k3, k3 from dpn. (Use for Strip 4)

C6L = Cable Left: Sl 3 sts to dpn and hold in front, k3, k3 from dpn. (Use for Strip 2)

Row 1 and all WS rows: K5, p6, k4, p6, k5.

Rows 2, 6, 8, 12: K.

Rows 4 and 10: K5, (C6R or C6L), k4, (C6R or C6L), k5.

Row 12: K.

Repeat rows 1–12 a total of 5 times.

BLOCK V (20 sts and 68 rows)

Rows 1–5: Knit.

Rows 6 and 8 (WS): K2, p16, k2.

Row 7: Knit.

Repeat rows 1–8 a total of 8 times, then work rows 1–4 again.

FLOPPY PILLOW

SIZE 18" x 18" / 45 x 45cm

Make 5 pieces, 1 in each color as follows:
Cast on 48 sts. K 8 rows.

Next row (RS): K.

Next row: K6, p12, k12, p12, k6.

Rep last 2 rows until piece measures 5",
end RS row. K7 rows. Bind off knitwise.

FINISHING Fold each piece in half and sew
2 sides. Use Seaming Method 2 on page 10.
Stuff and sew rem side. Sew pieces together
as indicated in photograph.

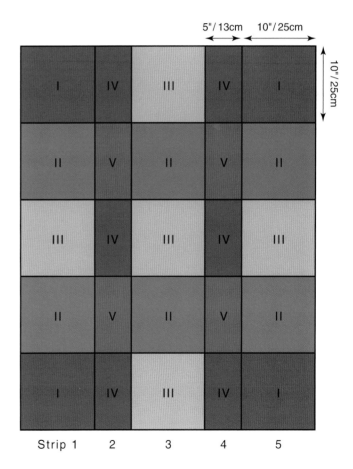

Friendship

SIZE 33" x 31" / 83 x 78cm

MATERIALS Manos Del Uruguay. Knitting needles size 9US / 5.5mm *or size to obtain given gauge*. Crochet hook H / 5mm for edging. Bobbins.

	Color	skns
A.	Powder C	2
B.	Natural 14	1
C.	Cheek 17	1
D.	Parma 20	1
E.	Cirrus 39	1
F.	Rose O	1
G.	Persimmon W	1
H.	Heather 50	1

NOTE When changing colors, use a separate bobbin of yarn for each block of color. Twist yarns on WS to prevent holes in work.

GAUGE 16 sts and 22 rows to 4" / 10 cm in St st.

BLOCK 1 With E, cast on 64 sts. K 4 rows. Work in vertical stripes as follows: **Next row (RS):** Work 4 sts C in **Garter**, the next 56 sts in **St st** as follows: 12 sts F, 11 sts A, 11 sts C, 11 sts A, 11 sts F; work rem 4 sts C in **Garter**. Cont as established for a total of 54 rows above border. With E, k 4 rows. Bind off.

BLOCK 2 With A, cast on 64 sts. K 4 rows. **Next row (RS):** Work 4 sts A in **Garter**, 56 sts of chart, 4 sts A in **Garter**. Cont as established until chart is completed. With A, k 4 rows. Bind off.

BLOCK 3 With D, cast on 64 sts. K 4 rows. **Next row (RS):** Work 4 sts D in **Garter**, 56 sts of chart, 4 sts D in **Garter**. Cont as established, working 4 Garter sts each side matching the background color of stripes on chart, until chart is completed. With D, k 4 rows. Bind off.

BLOCK 4 With H, cast on 64 sts. K 4 rows. **Next row (RS):** Work 4 sts in **Garter**, (use E for 4 rows, then change to A and work for rem rows), 56 sts of chart, 4 sts A in **Garter**. Cont as established until chart is completed. With A, k 4 rows. Bind off.

BLOCK 5 With F, cast on 64 sts. K 4 rows. **Next row (RS):** Keeping first and last 4 sts in **Garter** and center 56 sts in **St st**, work in foll stripes: 8 rows F, 7 rows C, 4 rows B, 5 rows E, 6 rows F, 5 rows E, 4 rows B, 7 rows C, 8 rows F. With F, k 4 rows. Bind off.

BLOCK 6 With A, cast on 64 sts and k 4 rows. **Next row (RS):** Work 4 sts A in **Garter**, 56 sts of chart, 4 sts A in **Garter**. Cont as established until chart is completed. With A, k 4 rows. Bind off.

FINISHING

Block each piece. Sew Blocks 1, 2 and 3 together into a vertical strip. Sew blocks 4, 5, and 6 together into another vertical strip. Sew strips together, using Seaming Method 2 shown on page 10. **Edging:** With crochet hook and B, work 1 rnd sc around outside edge of blanket. Work 1 rnd **Shrimp St**. Fasten off.

BLOCK 2

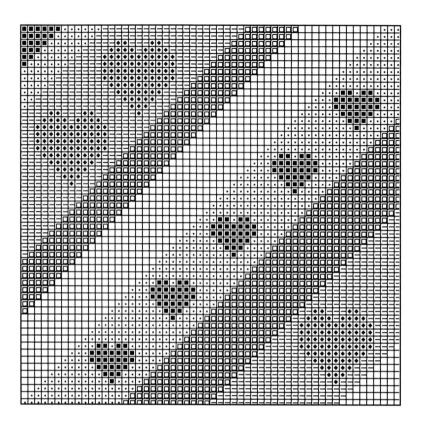

—	= Powder C
◢	= Natural 14
▪	= Cheek 17
☐	= Parma 20
☐	= Cirrus 39
■	= Rose O
⬛	= Persimmon W
✦	= Heather 50

BLOCK 3

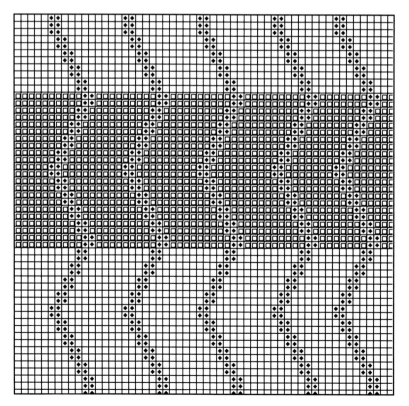

BLOCK 4

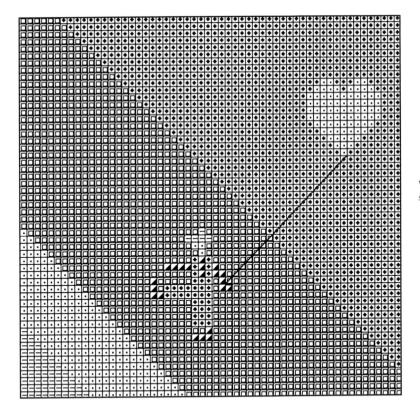

With A, embroider back-stitch for balloon string

BLOCK 6

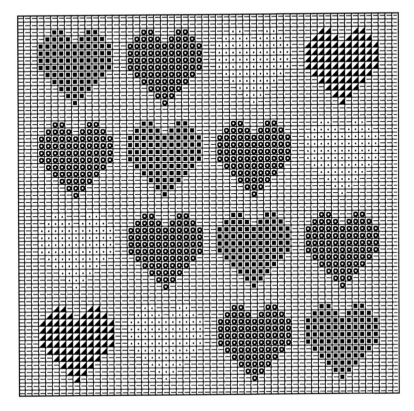

TRIBAL, p.31

FLOPPY, p.53

FELTED, p.62

SAUSAGE, p.61

KNITTED FLOWER, p.61

CIRCLES & SQUARES, p.60

TASSELED PILLOW, p.62

CROCHETED FLOWERS, p.61

Pillows

Pillows are a great way to use up odds and ends. I have indicated colorways to inspire you, but play with what you have, and if you run out of a color, don't hesitate to add in a new one.

PILLOW LINERS

MATERIALS 2 pieces of fabric same size as knitted piece plus 1 inch. Use a complimentary color as you may see it through the knitting. Washable stuffing material or pillow form.

LINER Pin knitted piece to 2 layers of fabric. Trace and cut out shape leaving ½" seam allowance all around. With right sides of fabric facing, sew seams, leaving one side open. Turn right side out, stuff and stitch remaining seam.

CIRCLES & SQUARES

SIZE 14" x 14" / 35 x 35cm

MATERIALS Manos del Uruguay, small amounts of assorted colors. 1 skein for back of pillow. Crochet hook J / 6mm.
Colors used in sample:

A. Rosin 26 (back)　　E.　Petrol 27
B. Spruce D　　　　　F.　Parma 20
C. Mint 18　　　　　　G.　Heather 50
D. Blush 24

CIRCLE (MAKE 9)

Foundation: 6ch, [dc, 2ch] 7 times into first ch of ch-6. Sl st to 4th ch of ch-6 – 8 spaces.

Rnd 1: Sl st into first sp, [3ch, 2dc] into same sp, [1ch, 3dc into next sp] 7 times. 1ch, sl st into 3rd ch of beg ch-3. Cut yarn and pull through loop.

SQUARE (MAKE 16)

Foundation: 5ch, join with sl st to first ch to form ring.

Rnd 1: 5ch (count as 1dc and 2ch), [3dc into ring, 2ch] 3 times, 2dc into ring, sl st to 3rd of ch-5.

Rnd 2: Sl st into next sp, 5ch, 3dc into same sp, [1ch, 3dc, 2ch, 3dc into next sp] 3 times. 1ch, 2dc into same sp as ch-5 at beg of rnd, sl st to 3rd ch of ch-5. Cut yarn and pull end through loop.

PILLOW BACK Work rnds 1 and 2 as for small square. Cont to work 10 more rnds as follows: Sl st into next sp, 5ch, 3dc into same sp, work [1ch, 3dc] into each sp along side to corner, work [1ch, 3dc, 2ch, 3dc] into each corner, end 1ch, 2dc into same sp as ch-5 at beg of rnd, sl st to 3rd ch of ch-5.

FINISHING Use Seaming Method 3 on pg 10. Sew circles together where they touch. Sew small squares together. Sew squares to circles. Sew 3 sides of back to front. Make pillow liner. Insert and sew remaining seam.

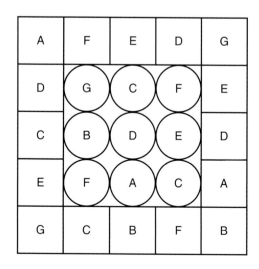

SAUSAGE

SIZE 24" / 60cm long x 18" / 45cm around

MATERIALS Manos del Uruguay. Small amts of 6 colors.
Needles 9US / 5.5 mm.
Colors use in sample:

A. Thrush 37	**D.** Shale 25
B. Mulberry 53	**E.** Bing Cherry M
C. Oil slick 34	**F.** Rosin 26

Note: *Only 6 colors were used in sample. Substitute one of the 6 colors for color G in* **Tribal Throw** *directions.*

Work as for Tribal Throw, page 29, working rows 1–94. Cont to work rows 95–188, dec 1 st at the end of each row. Block piece to measure 18" / 45cm square. With E, RS facing, pick up 72 sts along side edge A. **Rows 1–6:** K. **Rows 7 and 9 (WS):** P. **Row 8:** K. **Rows 10–13:** K. **Row 14:** K1, *yo, k2 tog; rep from *, end k1. **Row 15:** P. **Rows 16–19:** K. **Rows 20–25:** *K2, p2; rep from *. Bind off in rib pat. Rep on side edge B. With E, RS facing, pick up 72 sts along edge C. K 1 row, sl sts to another needle. Rep along edge D. With wrong sides tog and right side facing, k seam tog as follows: K first st from front needle tog with first st from back needle, *k next st from front and back needles tog, sl first st over 2nd st to bind off; rep from * until all sts are bound off. Cut yarn and slip end through rem st. Sew seams X and Y. **Ropes (make 2):** Cut 4 pieces color A, each 48" / 120cm long. Tie together at one end with an overhand knot. Hook end to something stationary. With 2 ends in each hand, follow directions for fringe on page 30. Weave rope through eyelets at each end of pillow. Pull one end tight and tie in bow. Insert pillow liner and tie other end.

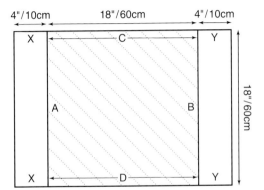

SAUSAGE PILLOW LINER

Cut fabric 25" x 20" / 63 x 50cm

Fold over 1½" / 4cm at ends A and B and stitch in place. Thread 24" / 60cm piece of yarn or string through each end. With right sides facing, sew edges C and D together. Turn right side out. Pull string at one end tight. Stuff and pull other end tight.

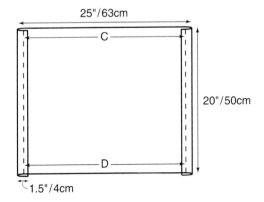

FLOWER PILLOWS

SIZE Approx 10" / 25cm across

MATERIALS Manos del Uruguay, approx. 12 yds per hexagon. 2 buttons for knitted version.

HEXAGONS See pages 14 and 16 for crocheted and knitted directions. Work 14 hexagons (7 per side) for each pillow as shown in diagrams. Work knitted version in 3 strips. Colors may be reversed for other side of pillow. **Finishing:** Sew crocheted pieces together using Seaming Method 3 on page 10; sew knitted strips together using Method 1. Sew side seams, leaving opening for pillow liner. Make pillow liner and insert. Stitch remaining sides. **Knitted version:** Sew 1 button on each side, pulling thread tightly through center of pillow several times.

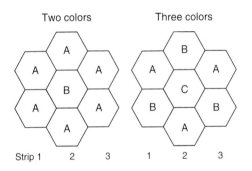

FELTED PILLOW

FINISHED SIZE Approx. 10" x 17" / 25 x 45cm

PRE-FELTED SIZE Approx. 13" x 27" / 33 x 68cm

MATERIALS Manos del Uruguay, 1 skn color A, 2 skns color B. 26" circular needle no. 10½ / 6.5mm. 6 1¼" / 3mm buttons. *Pillow shown in colors Bing Cherry M (A) and Cinnamon V (B).*

GAUGE 14 sts = 4" / 10cm in St st

Button Border: With A, cast on 92 sts. Join and mark beg of rnds. *K 8 rnds. **Next rnd (buttonholes):** K7, [bind off 5, k next 8 sts] twice, bind off 5, k rem sts. **Next rnd:** K, cast on 5 sts at each buttonhole. K 8 more rnds.* Cut A. **Center area:** With B, k all rnds until you run out of yarn. Cut B. With A, work button border from * to *. Bind off.

FELTING Set washing machine to hot wash, cold rinse. Mix in 1 tsp of dishwashing liquid. Let pillow go through 1 cycle. Shape and lay flat to dry.

FINISHING Sew on buttons. Measure center area of pillow. Make pillow liner this size and insert.

TASSELED PILLOW

SIZE 18" x 18" / 45 x 45cm

MATERIALS Manos Del Uruguay, 1 skn each:

A. Juniper 43

B. Aster 38

C. Lapis 45

D. Raspberry 57

Knitting needles size 9US / 5.5mm. Crochet hook H / 4.75mm.

Work 2 strips as follows:

STRIP 1

With color A, cast on 52 sts. K 2 rows. Work **Block 1**, page 34, as follows: **Next row (RS):** Work 3 sts in **Garter**, 46 sts in **Double Moss**, 3 sts in **Garter**. Cont in pats as established until block measures 12¾" / 32.5cm, end with WS row. K 2 rows.

With color B, k 2 rows. Work **Block 2**, page 34, as follows: **Next row (RS):** Work 3 sts in **Garter**, 46 sts in **Beaded Rib**, 3 sts in **Garter**. Cont in pats as established until block measures 12¾" / 31.5cm, end with WS row. K 2 rows. Bind off knitwise.

STRIP 2

With color C, cast on 52 sts. K 2 rows, inc 2 sts evenly across last row – 54 sts. Work **Block 12**, page 37, as follows: **Next row (RS):** Work 3 sts **Garter**, 48 sts in **Basket**, 3 sts **Garter**. Cont in pats as established until block measures 12¾" / 32.5cm, end with WS row. K2 rows, dec 2 sts evenly across first row – 52 sts.

With color D, k 2 rows. Work **Block 4**, page 34, as follows: Work 3 sts **Garter**, 46 sts **St st/Garter rib**, 3 sts **Garter**. Cont. in pats as established until block measures 12¾" / 31.5cm, end with WS row. K 2 rows. Bind off knitwise.

FINISHING Sew strips tog as shown in diagram, using Seaming Method 2 on page 10. Fold 3 corner points into center and sew seams. Make pillow liner and insert. Fold in rem corner. With crochet hook and matching colors, start at corners and join remaining 2 seams with a row of sc. Make 4 tassels, 1 in each color, and attach to corners. To remove liner for cleaning, undo crocheted seams.

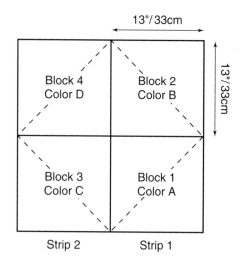

Friendship Throw was originally knitted as a baby present for Anne Simpson when her first child, Chris, was born. Six of her sales representatives knitted a block each. Everyone worked with the same color selection, but the designs were created individually.

EGS Throw was designed by Anne Simpson, inspired by one her mother, Elizabeth Gruber Simpson, knit for Anne's sister to take to college.

Harvest Throw designed by Anne Simpson

Amish Throw designed by Liza Prior Lucy

All other designs by Judith Shangold

Book design by Judith Shangold

Instructions edited by Janice Bye

Knitters: Kim Barnett, Janice Bye, Joan Cassidy, Elaine Mei, Charlotte Fruciano, and the knitters from Manos del Uruguay.

Technical drawings, production, and general consultations by Steve Dyer

Photography by Atlantic Photo

I would especially like to acknowledge Anne Simpson, who was the U.S. distributor of Manos del Uruguay from 1986 to 1999. With her tasteful eye for color and design, Anne developed many beautiful design collections that established Manos as a popular handknitting yarn. Over the years, I worked with Anne as one of her sales representatives and contributing designers, and we became good friends. When she decided to retire from this business to spend more time with her family, she offered me the opportunity to assume the Manos distributorship. I am thrilled to have this opportunity to build on the solid foundation that Anne created.

Judith Shangold

My special thanks to my husband, Steve Dyer, who provided his professional skills, and spent seemingly endless hours helping me pore over these pages. I thank him for his fine eye, his attention to detail, and his patience with me and this project.

Manos del Uruguay yarn and books are distributed by

DESIGN SOURCE

PO Box 770, Medford MA 02155

781-438-9631   888-566-9970

Judith Shangold, owner

Distributor of patterns from

MINNOWKNITS™ by Jil Eaton

A BEAR IN SHEEP'S CLOTHING

DESIGNS BY JUDITH